T0193912

GOD'S
BEST FOR ME AND YOU!

JANE FRANCES ANDERSEN

WESTBOW
PRESS®
A DIVISION OF THOMAS NELSON
& ZONDERVAN

WestBow Press books may be ordered through booksellers or by contacting:

WestBow Press
A Division of Thomas Nelson & Zondervan
1663 Liberty Drive
Bloomington, IN 47403
www.westbowpress.com
1 (866) 928-1240

ISBN: 978-1-5127-8226-4 (sc)
ISBN: 978-1-5127-8225-7 (e)

Library of Congress Control Number: 2017905263

Print information available on the last page.

WestBow Press rev. date: 04/11/2017

DEDICATION

This book is dedicated to my loving, supportive husband, Henry, and for all to be healed and find Jesus in their lives.

TABLE OF CONTENTS

CHAPTER 1

We have a loving God, the Triune God. I think first of all his qualities is Love. And I did go through things to learn something or develop something within me. It's all been for the best when I look back on it. He led me through the darkness to His wonderful light, or I was living in the Light and found darkness around me. But it's all been for the best. The best for me, the Best from God.

I'm 69 years old almost and I found that I never lacked anything. I had what I needed. When I found Jesus after a serious illness at 22 years of age, I knew I wanted to follow Him and do His will. I didn't want sin in my life. And I see when there was sin, not doing God's will, there were results or consequences to those sins for it wasn't God's best for me.

But God didn't give up on me. He forgave me and strengthened me to follow Him more closely through the years.

There is the Pharisee and the Publican. The Pharisee said "I'm thankful I am so good and not as this poor Publican." But the Publican said, "God forgive me my sins" and beat his breast. God favored the Publican.

I think there comes a time when someone will tell us we've made a mistake, and we need those people. Although at the time we think they should mind their own business or "are they perfect?" But we need correction. Wouldn't you rather have a loving mother or father or both tell you when you're wrong? I would. And God is that parent of all His children. We need to listen from the Lord.

And then repent of our misbehavior, a turn around, and be forgiven, so we can grow In Christ.

And wouldn't our Creator know what's best for us and what we need to or truly desire for us to be? Some times I remember my flimsy plans and thankfully abandoned them for God's will. And it was wonderful, the results of doing God's will and following Him.

God is a correcting, punishing God; but He does so out of pure Love. Love is His greatest attribute.

Don't you see that if you do anything you want without the counsel of God, that it leads to destruction? We need the correction of Our Loving God, our Loving Parent.

I'm thankful my parents corrected me and disciplined me. Otherwise, it leads to destruction.

And I am saved from destruction and for Eternal Life.

CHAPTER 2

Now I feel that God loves me, I must in turn love myself and treat myself with respect, and leave unkind, abusive people alone. They always have something to offer me, that's how I got involved to begin with. Then I learned that I can be independent of them and go on without them.

Things happen to you and you don't want it to. But somehow at the time it's out of our control to stop it, or we are just too young and inexperienced or immature to put a stop to it. But somehow with time and experience we gain the strength to stop it.

Caught up in the abuse, somehow we think it's our fault or we start abusing ourselves, too, thinking we are worthless if we're treated by someone that way. But we are worth a lot to God and to humanity. And we find that it's not important what these people think (and they are stupid in some ways) and find what God thinks is important for He loves us and made us valuable and undeserving of mistreatment.

During that time of abuse and feeling very bad we start using food or whatever (I used food) to heal our pain. Then there's addiction and another problem to solve.

Then we realize that we can lean on God and He will help us. But it seems like there's still a temptation to relieve our tensions and ill feelings with food.

Then there's a weight problem. But it's not the problem, it's only a symptom of a problem. The problem is hurt.

There's help out there in the world, and we need some kind of patience with ourselves, too. Things don't always cure overnight. It's two steps forward and one step back.

Dealing with others in 12 Step programs can help a lot. There always seems like someone there understands you and can help you overcome.

I went to Emotions Anonymous (EA), Overeaters Anonymous (OA), and Codependents Anonymous (CoDa).

They all helped but Emotions Anonymous did the most good. When dealing with your overeating, codependency, and other issues, then you have your emotions to deal with. So Emotions Anonymous is the Masters Degree of anonymous groups. For there's always the emotions.

And it's not a bunch of crazy people. They are sensible people with problems to deal with and willing to get help. Never seeing getting help a weakness. It's a strength.

Somehow we get messed up in this world and need help to get out of the mess.

And then with all of that help, we can start to help ourselves, start being our own advocate. Our own best friend.

There are books that can help you with that. I hope this one will, and many others.

CHAPTER 3

Watch what you listen to, it can be a blessing or it can be a curse. We are affected by many people in our lives. Mom and Dad mostly, and then on from there. We learn and either feel good or bad about it. And we all want to feel good. But sometimes that isn't easy for us to have those good feelings.

Sometimes we choose food, alcohol, or whatever to "feel good" again. And that works against us, too. And end up feeling worse. My addiction (wanting to feel good) was and is food. We all need food, but it can be an addiction. And it seems like the weight gain cannot be lost after it's gained.

I read all the books (or plenty of them) on diet, weight loss, food addiction. I learned quite a bit but I'm still heavy. And you watch all those "success" stories and you think you can be one, too. So, you buy the weight loss product. And then you try and then you fail. And end up feeling like a failure too, yet.

And it first started with listening to the destructive criticism out there. The degrading words you definitely don't need to hear. So, then I've got to get my head straightened out and try to get some kind of healthy self esteem for myself.

It's hard for me, but I've got to realize the words people use is because maybe they're not happy with themselves either and influence you to feel the same.

I'm more of a passive person. Just take the abuse. I feel what's the use of standing up for myself. You can't win. But I realize I must find a way to win and regain my lost self esteem.

And not be influenced by these people.

And how important are these people's opinions to you? Are they some kind of authority figure or sick dependency of yours? Maybe God lets these people in your life to teach you. Teach you to be more your own person and be independent. At least independent of them.

And sometimes certain counselors come to an end, for you've outgrown them. It may be time to move on, with someone else, or one more step to depend on yourself.

And we've got to learn to be dependable to ourselves.

Remember there's some control freaks out there. They feel good by controlling you. When they lose their power over you, you deflate their egos. One friend said, "bust their egos."

CHAPTER 4

Your emotions can help you solve a bothersome problem. I was feeling so bad emotionally, I didn't know how to solve my problems, and felt and felt and felt. And then I turned to food to feel better. And that was a mistake, for it's a drug, my drug of choice.

Then I ballooned up. And then I had to face the disgrace of being fat and at that time it was a thin world.

But your emotions are there for a reason. And finally I did learn how to solve my problems by listening to myself. The emotions didn't go away fast, but eventually they subsided. Healing can be in an instant or gradually you can get well. Three steps forward and two steps back isn't all that bad. It's progress.

I finally learned how to take care of myself and not let other people "take charge." You "take charge" and not be a victim.

Emotions can make you tired, too. It takes away from your energies. Sometimes when I was angry, I felt a surge of energy (adrenaline) and then soon afterward, I was exhausted and depressed. Depression is anger turned inward.

Emotions can wear you out.

We are emotional beings.

CHAPTER 5

Your self esteem can be affected by people's remarks and by problems you don't know how to solve effectively.

When my self esteem went down, my weight shot up. One friend said, "don't let people destroy your self esteem." And I watch that kind of thing like a hawk now. It's like radar out watching for people who might erode my self respect.

And people have their negative opinion about you, but why respect their horrible opinion? They aren't to be respected.

Why respect what people think when they are people you don't like?

To sum it up: they're stupid!

CHAPTER 6

Remember, especially today, there's help out there. Let people teach you something. We don't know it all and we can always learn something new which is helpful to our healing.

Lots of people came to my rescue during those hard times. My mind was on the unkind people, but as I got well I realized that there are some pretty good people out there in the world, too. Helpful people, healing people, people that have gone through the same thing or similar with the same kind of emotions to deal with.

Some people have been hurt and healed and that is their mission to help the people still suffering. They are your assets.

There's 12 step groups, ministers (Christian), psychologists, psychiatrists. Whatever you do, get a good one. There are some unwise or unkind counselors out there, too. Who can do more harm than good.

And if you reach out, you find you're not alone or different from everyone else.

And with their help, you learn you can help yourself, too.

CHAPTER 7

Be your own advocate. Help yourself, too. Don't kick yourself when you're down. Learn to be there for yourself.

You are a child of God and valuable to Him, and then with His help, you can be helpful to yourself, and then, maybe, for others, too.

Sometimes with our problems, we learn to be our own worst enemy. And that can be devastating. You can learn to love yourself, faults and all, too. Sometimes, just love yourself first. And then it's not so hard to love others.

For a long while, I was so good to others, and not to myself. That was unfair. I needed to balance that love for myself and others.

CHAPTER 8

F ear can be overwhelming at times, panic attacks were frequent in my life. And they'd come on with not much prodding. Nothing much set them off.

I found out much later that I had an inner child in me, and it was scared to death. Then I learned to be some kind of parent to it and support this vulnerable part of me.

Comfort, nurture, and protect this inner child.

CHAPTER 9

Comfort, nurture, and protect this inner child. If you put it in others' hands, that's how you get caught up with "sick dependencies."

And these people "feel good" by controlling you sometimes. Most always.

Learn to be your own person and run your own life. You know something, too. And don't be vulnerable to other people who are control freaks.

When they're jealous, that can be a double whammy.

And they're not interested in you succeeding. Contrary. They want you to fail.

And they hook you with something to "help" you. You think they're helping you, but they're not at all. Be independent of their good will before having to "cope" with them.

CHAPTER 10

Have boundaries. People don't respect people who don't have boundaries. You must know where some people can go in your life and where they can't go.

Different people need different boundaries. You wouldn't tell a gossip some private business. But a trusted, confidential friend you could. And some people you would say "hello" to, but some you might invite over for dinner. And this is a personal one, but who would you allow in your bed?

And I do believe in sexual purity, for where do you draw the line with some people? Don't let people "use" you.

Say NO. No is a powerful word.

CHAPTER 11

God brings the best in us through another's illness or disability, especially in the family. My husband Henry has health problems. Usually it's real easy for me for he's congenial with everything.

He started to have heart problems and needed to be run back and forth to the hospital. At first I felt powerless for I'm such a bad driver, bad on directions.

Then I realize that I could get there but finding parking was hard. And I'd get confused which lot to turn into.

So, you get one thing down pat and then another thing arises.

And I was listening to a radio program on Christian radio. And it talked about grief of a loss of a loved one. Which I may have to endure some day but I hope not soon.

We're turning 70 and it's time for some of us get really ill or die. But I firmly believe "let the problems of the day be enough for today." And live in "daytight" compartments. Only today. That's all I can handle.

And remember God only gives you what you can endure. And there's something to learn from every experience. When we get out of our comfort zone, sometimes it's good.

And my independence arises the more I'm left to things myself.

CHAPTER 12

I must remember that I am and others are cracked pots. We are earthen vessels and sometimes we crack.

I know I fudged up on certain relationships by being myself. For at the time, I wasn't doing so good. I had stress and unhappiness and negative people hurting me and controlling me. I couldn't be that "happy" Jane at the time. And I hurt the people I most admire and love. I didn't want to be that way, though. I didn't rejoice in it. I regret the unkind things I said forever.

But we must forgive ourselves and move on. And hope they don't hold it against us forever. I hope they won't.

And I must realize other people are cracked pots, too. They aren't the best to us for they are going through turmoil and unhappiness, too. Sometimes we want people always to be their best. Sometimes they can do that for us, and most of the time they can't. Just like we can't.

So we must forgive their indifference and unkindnesses, too.

And sometimes some people aren't what we want in friends, too. They just don't have kindness, understanding, and love for us. And we don't need that.

And some people never change. People go through hard times and learn to be different, but some people just choose to be "stinkers."

And we must remember, those people don't realize the way they are. It's beyond them to see that for themselves.

CHAPTER 13

There is tiredness we have to cope with at times. Emotions can make you tired, anger, depression which is anger gone inward, and other emotions. Nervousness makes you tired. And getting older makes you tired. (Stress wears me out.)

So, the solution mostly is just rest. Rest, rest. Good sleep can make things all better. And then when you're refreshed, you can go and do the work God intends for you.

And when you solve bothersome problems, you get serenity or peace about things. A new confidence in yourself, too. We've got to solve our problems but it must be in God's way, in His Word. And two wrongs don't make a right. We've got to do it God's way, which is the best way, with the best results. For you and others.

We don't need to accept the abuse of others. If you accept it, they think they can get by with it and don't respect you. Let people know you are not to be walked on. Respect yourself enough to stand up to them. And let them go on with somebody else. They are enemies. And please, don't listen to them. Have a deaf ear to their put downs.

Putting up with these people can make you angry and tired. Pray to God that He will deliver you from the power of your enemies.

You can be helpless only so long. And then you will take care of yourself with these people.

And the easiest solution but not always possible is just staying away from them.

Always try to eat nutritious meals, too. And usually that's eating at home. Fast food and restaurant take out and gas station food is usually not the healthiest for you. And eating poorly can make you sick and tired. And that affects your emotions, too. But we can do only the best we can do and that's it, and sometimes we have to take the easy way, too. So, it's never perfect this nutrition stuff.

Eat right, rest, and stay away from what hurts you. These things are always good for you.

CHAPTER 14

I guess I'm getting where I want to be, more self-contained. Keep things to myself more. "only a fool blurts out everything he knows," it says in Proverbs.

And independence is a good thing as long as you're not independent of God. We need Him, don't think we don't. That's where everything comes from to supply this body and life.

I admit I was helpless with some "toxic" people. They ruled and controlled me. But that was for just a little while. Then my self respect rose and I ousted them in my life for good. And I did learn some lessons from those sick dependencies.

One thing I leaned on, which was not good, was food. I ate for comfort and to ease my "stress." I ate to "feel good." But it all taught me to "feel my feelings" and "help myself."

The inner child in you is defenseless in a world like this. We need to be a good parent with good reasoning to help ourselves. If we can't, we're in trouble. And no one needs trouble. It can make you sick. In other words we need to love ourselves like a loving mother would.

And the fear rose in me being helpless years ago. And the fear was a blessing, too. It taught me something was wrong with my life. Some way I needed to learn and grow and "take charge."

We've got to be our own best friend in that way. We need that control.

CHAPTER 15

Suffering isn't all bad. It's true, it's no picnic. But maybe a picnic isn't what we needed at the time. We needed to learn and grow from suffering. At least we know what to stay away from the "next time."

I had a breakdown of emotional health at 18 years of age. And it lasted for a few years. During those years, I had no parties, I had no job, no good times with friends. In fact, friends were few. They that fled didn't want a "sick" person for a friend because that's no fun. They wanted their good times, and I had my bad times.

But the sickness those years kept me away from outside employment which the Lord, in later years, wanted me to stay home with my child and my house to keep. And now I know that's all I could do. I couldn't be a working mom coming home after a "hard day's" work and do for my family. I didn't have the strength. God knew best. And even though things were taken from me, the inability to be in the workforce, illness, God gave me His best.

And those years of "good times" were occasions to sin. And God kept me out of all that sin. Sexual and otherwise. I believe in sexual purity and not giving yourself away, only to your husband or wife. And my husband believes that, too. Of course, we've had our temptations and "pullings" but didn't give in to such stuff.

God gives us His best by protecting us, too. Sometimes with suffering and adversity.

CHAPTER 16

I had my 70th birthday yesterday. Henry and I went out to eat at Crusoe's in South St. Louis. Henry gave me a necklace and earring set in my birthstone, Garnet. And Scott, our son, came over and gave me a tea kettle, a nice one. I had a blessed time.

God doesn't always give you affliction to be good to you. He gives you good times, too.

I got a few birthday cards. And on Facebook, I received so many, many good wishes.

God sends you friends through the years.

When I was sickly, friends were few. I understand their view of me, but it was not nice of them to leave me. But it was a good time spent with the Lord and a couple of abiding friends who showed me mercy and kindness, and patience. It was a hard time, but it was a good time, too.

Now I enjoy health and peace. And now I appreciate things more.

CHAPTER 17

God gives us our gifts. Be thankful and treasure every one of them. I got a good start (and I will finish well) with good Godly parents. I will always treasure their kindness, unconditional love, and, yes, correction (for we all need it).

Mom and Dad didn't just go to church. They had Jesus as their personal Savior. They followed after God and made Him first. He was their first love.

And I came to Jesus, too. In 1969 after a long illness (4 years). I accepted Jesus and my miracle healing.

And I am forever blest with such parents. I set them on a high pedestal.

We had a life of peace and love. But having that didn't bring me to Jesus. I had "through much trial and tribulation enter the kingdom of God." For God has no grandkids. He only has His children. When I became a young adult, I came to Christ.

And I've walked with Jesus ever since.

But I still wish that today I still had my mom and dad to love and correct me. I am 70 and they've been gone for quite a few years. Gone to heaven, and waiting for me to come, too, someday.

CHAPTER 18

During my stressful and unhappy illness in the late 1960's, I developed easing my hurts with food. And as I did that, I became a compulsive overeater. Many years later I went to Overeaters Anonymous, telling me that it is an illness that needs to be arrested.

Before that, and after, too, I read all the diet books. I went to Weight Watchers and Tops, Inc., too. I lost at Weight Watchers and didn't at Tops. But it didn't take away my addiction to food.

I bought books on Food Addiction, different ones. And it seems like the addiction was more about sugar than anything else. So, that's one thing I am cautious of.

When Jesus was on the cross with great cruelty and suffering, they offered him wine on a stick in a sponge. But he refused it. When I suffered much, I took the candy bar, or bars. Then I became hooked on something that would relieve my suffering. But also created another problem, addiction to sugar and weight gain.

I'd see the commercials at that time on TV and it was like I was very attracted to the food and junk food shown and sold on them. And I would starve myself because I knew I was out of control. And my mom said I was a different person when I ate those foods. It affected my mood. And I turned cruel on myself, not accepting myself anymore. For now I was fat. And I knew I was out of control.

So, the addiction stopped me from loving myself anymore. I was in a state of illness and addiction.

But when I came to Jesus, I found His love and could love myself more, but I was still hard on myself.

In the psyche ward in the hospital, they put me on a 1200 calorie diet and I lost it all. I stayed thin until I had a baby after being married. Then there were a whole new set of problems, not the child's fault, though. It came from a cruel, manipulating, control freak of a mother in law.

I finally, after 12 years of her abuse, broke free from her control. I went to Emotions Anonymous and realized I could stay away and be free of such abuse. And say "no" to her. They taught me how to take care of myself.

Emotions Anonymous is a 12 Step group.

There was stress and different difficulties at that time, too. I realized that I was codependent. And realized I let other people control me, wanting their acceptance and love. And letting things happen to me that I shouldn't of let happen. Even if it was only emotions, I got sick from those dependencies. So, a wonderful girlfriend said to go to Codependents Anonymous. And I read some of the literature and books on the subject, and my eyes were opened.

Sometimes it's not just denial or it isn't that. You just don't know what the problem is until you are ready to be shown and someone shows you. An alcoholic said "I had to be shown." I couldn't figure it out for myself or alone. I needed help, and I got it.

CHAPTER 19

Take the best and "leave" the rest. Stay away from what harms you. Be strong and courageous and listen to all the Lord Jesus and God says in His Word. The Bible.

There's always "payoffs" to destructive relationships. You have to "let go" of the payoffs and release yourself from the destructive relationship.

You know how to "catch a monkey?" Take a hollow coconut and put a hole in it, the size of a monkey to reach in, but not big enough to let the hand out if it's clutching candy. And put candy in it, so the monkey reaches for the candy and won't "let go." So, his hand is stuck in the coconut. And that's how to catch a monkey. He won't let go of the candy.

That's how the Devil catches us. Gives us something dangerous and destructive and keeps us in the relationship with something attractive or we are dependent on it. And we can't let go because we want that or are dependent on it.

And with some people, "be independent of their goodwill, before having to cope with them."

CHAPTER 20

GOD WANTS HIS BEST, YOUR BEST, FOR YOU, TOO!

When you were conceived, God had a plan for your life. An eternal future with Him, and the every day stuff that comes up on earth.

It takes a while sometimes to come to God or find Him. But when you do, you are born again. And your walk with the Lord begins. You can't reason it; it's a childlike faith. Unless you come to God like a child, you cannot enter the kingdom of heaven.

We learn more about God and His love for us in the Holy Bible, His Word. It's God inspired. We learn more about what he commands in our life by reading it regularly. And we learn the consequences of our disobedience for He wants us to avoid trouble in our lives. Trouble can make you sick and/or unhappy.

We are made to love, obey, and serve Him. Now and forevermore. That's GOD'S BEST!

I hope you benefited from my testimony. I wish that you would come to Jesus and be born again, as I am. It's not an easy life, but it's a blessed life. And that you will be saved (that begins when you are "born again."), and repent of your sins (for all have sinned and come short of the glory of God.) And follow Jesus, and he will make you "fishers of men." For God wants all to be saved and come to the knowledge of the truth. JESUS IS THE WAY, THE TRUTH, AND THE LIFE.

Hope to see you in heaven next to the throne of God, worshipping Him forever and ever in our glorified bodies.

GOD'S BLESSINGS, Jane.

Printed in the United States
By Bookmasters